D1518898

Harbor Seals

by Ellen Lawrence

Consultant:

Kieran Copeland
Seal Care Supervisor
Hunstanton Sea Life Sanctuary
Hunstanton, England

BEARPORT
PUBLISHING

New York, New York

Credits

Cover, © mauribo/Istock Photo; 2, © Eric Isselee/Shutterstock; 4, © Ic66/Istock Photo; 5, © Ingo Arndt/Nature Picture Library; 6, © Bildagentur Zoonar GmbH/Shutterstock; 7, © Arterra Picture Library/Alamy; 8, © JpaulB/Istock Photo; 9, © Ernie Janes/ Nature Picture Library; 9TR, © Ken Canning/Istock Photo; 10, Kevin Ebi/Alamy; 11, © ImageBroker/FLPA; 12, © Roland Hemmi/ Design Pics/Getty Images; 13, © Douglas Klug/Getty Images; 14, © Cultura RM/Alamy; 15, © BehindTheLens/Istock Photo; 16, © jgareri/Istock Photo; 17, © BehindTheLens/Istock Photo; 18T, © Bildagentur Zoonar GmbH/Shutterstock; 18B, © Christian Musat/Shutterstock; 19T, © jennifer.sche/Shutterstock; 19, © Federica Grassi/Getty Images; 20, © Brett Cole Photography; 21, © mauribo/Istock Photo; 22L, © Suzi Eszterhas/Nature Picture Library; 22TR, © blickwinkel/Alamy; 22BR, © Arterra Picture Library/Alamy; 23TL, © Clare Louise Jackson/Shutterstock; 23TC, © Ulrike Jordan/Shutterstock; 23TR, © Kuttelvaserova Stuchelova/Shutterstock; 23BL, © Joel Sartore/Getty Images; 23BC, © Joe Blossom/Alamy; 23BR, © Vlada Photo/Shutterstock.

Publisher: Kenn Goin
Senior Editor: Joyce Tavolacci
Creative Director: Spencer Brinker
Photo Researcher: Ruth Owen Books

Library of Congress Cataloging-in-Publication Data

Names: Lawrence, Ellen, 1967– , author.
Title: Harbor seals / by Ellen Lawrence.
Description: New York, New York : Bearport Publishing, 2018. | Series: A day at the beach : animal life on the shore | Includes bibliographical references and index. | Audience: Ages 5 to 8.
Identifiers: LCCN 2017048988 (print) | LCCN 2017052123 (ebook) | ISBN 9781684025060 (Ebook) | ISBN 9781684024483 (library)
Subjects: LCSH: Harbor seal—Juvenile literature.
Classification: LCC QL737.P64 (ebook) | LCC QL737.P64 L39 2018 (print) | DDC 599.79/23—dc23
LC record available at https://lccn.loc.gov/2017048988

Copyright © 2018 Bearport Publishing Company, Inc. All rights reserved. No part of this publication may be reproduced in whole or in part, stored in any retrieval system, or transmitted in any form or by any means, electronic, mechanical, photocopying, recording, or otherwise, without written permission from the publisher.

For more information, write to Bearport Publishing Company, Inc., 45 West 21st Street, Suite 3B, New York, New York 10010. Printed in the United States of America.

10 9 8 7 6 5 4 3 2 1

Contents

Furry Sunbathers

It's a hot summer day at the seashore.

The beach is covered with hundreds of sunbathers.

At times, some of them splash into the water.

These beach visitors aren't people—they're harbor seals!

They have come ashore to rest and sun themselves.

When seals leave the water to rest on a beach or rocks, it's called hauling-out.

Meet a Harbor Seal

A harbor seal is a large ocean **mammal**.

An adult can weigh up to 230 pounds (104 kg) and be 6 feet (1.8 m) long!

Its fur has spots and may be white, gray, or brown.

The animal's skin produces oils that cover its spotty fur.

The oils make a seal's coat waterproof!

A harbor seal has large eyes for seeing in murky ocean water. Its eyeballs are covered with a layer of **mucus** that protects them underwater.

Every harbor seal has its own special pattern of spots.

Why do you think a harbor seal's fur pattern is helpful to scientists?
(The answer is on page 24.)

A Seal's World

Harbor seals got their name because they live close to beaches and **harbors**.

They don't usually swim more than 20 miles (32 km) from the shore.

These animals spend about half their lives in the water.

The other half is spent hauled-out on land in places known as rookeries.

a seal resting on floating ice

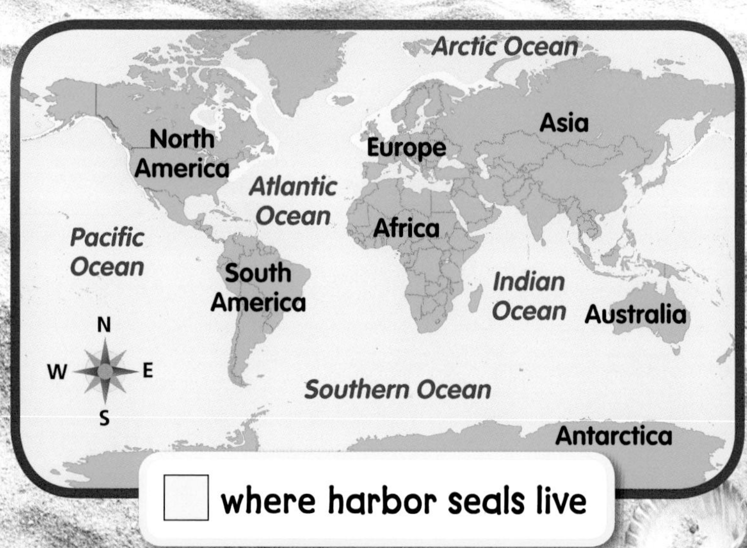

where harbor seals live

A harbor seal needs its own space. If another seal comes too close, it will growl and even smack its neighbor with its flippers.

Harbor seals often do something called galumphing. Can you guess what this is?

Galumphing!

Harbor seals like to splash and play in the ocean.

They roll, twist, and do somersaults!

Sometimes, they chase each other onto rocks or the beach.

Moving on land isn't easy for these large animals.

To get around, they bounce on their bellies!

seals playing

As it bounces on its belly, the seal's body makes wave-like movements to push it forward. This way of moving is called galumphing.

a harbor seal galumphing into the ocean

How do you think a seal's whiskers help it find food?

Diving for Dinner

Harbor seals dive deep underwater to find food.

They catch fish such as herrings, salmon, and sand eels.

They also eat small octopuses and squid.

The seal uses its sensitive whiskers to find its **prey** moving in the water.

Then it grabs the animal in its mouth and gobbles it down.

sand eel

Harbor seals can dive to depths of about 600 feet (183 m). They can stay underwater for up to 40 minutes.
whiskers

A Beach Baby

Once a year, male and female harbor seals meet up to **mate**.

About nine months later, a female seal gives birth to a pup.

The furry baby is born on the beach, along with lots of other pups.

Within an hour of being born, the little seal is ready to go swimming with its mom.

a harbor seal mother and pup

A newborn harbor seal weighs about 20 pounds (9 kg). That's about the same weight as a large watermelon!

mother seals
What do you think
a harbor seal pup eats?
pups

Being a Pup

A harbor seal pup drinks milk from its mother's body.

At first, the mother seal stays with her baby day and night.

After about 10 days, she must leave to find more food.

Sometimes, the pup goes with its mom, diving with her as she catches fish.

At other times, the pup waits for her on the beach.

a pup drinking milk
A mother seal's milk contains lots of fat. A pup gains more than 1 pound (0.5 kg) each day. After four weeks, it has doubled its weight!

Growing Up

When the pup is four weeks old, it's ready to take care of itself.

It spends its days swimming or resting on a beach.

In the ocean, a young seal must watch out for enemies such as orcas and sharks.

On land, there is danger from bears and coyotes.

If a predator on the beach gets too close to the pup, it galumphs into the water.

polar bear

orca

young seals galumphing into the sea

A seal can sleep on a beach—or in the sea! When taking an ocean nap, it floats upright with its head sticking out of the water.

a seal sleeping

Bad Hair Days

Once a seal is an adult, it will **molt** its coat each summer.

Molting helps keep the seal's skin and fur healthy.

It takes about six weeks for a seal's old fur to fall out.

Underneath, a new coat has grown.

The seal suns itself in its new spotted fur!

A harbor seal can live for up to 30 years. Most seals spend their lives near the beach where they were born.

Science Lab

Be a Harbor Seal Scientist!

We know a lot about harbor seals because scientists study them. Now it's your turn to investigate! Read the following questions and write your answers in a notebook.

1. What do you think is happening in this picture?

2. What do you think the seal is doing here?

3. Like most animals, harbor seals need water to survive. However, they can't drink salty seawater. Where do you think seals get the water they need?

(The answers are on page 24.)

Science Words

harbors (HAR-burz) bodies of water where ships can stay safe and unload goods

mammal (MAM-uhl) a warm-blooded animal that is covered with fur or hair and drinks its mother's milk as a baby

mate (MAYT) to come together to have young

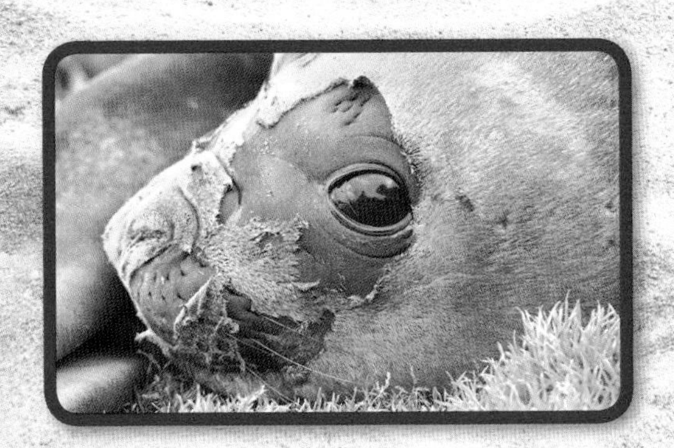

molt (MOHLT) to shed an outer covering of fur, feathers, or skin so a new covering can grow

mucus (MYOO-kuhss) a slimy liquid made by an animal

prey (PRAY) an animal that is eaten by another animal

Index

Read More

Hewett, Joan. *A Harbor Seal Pup Grows Up (Baby Animals).* Minneapolis, MN: Lerner (2002).

Owen, Ruth. *Seal Pups (Water Babies).* New York: Bearport (2013).

Spilsbury, Louise. *Seal (A Day in the Life: Sea Animals).* North Mankato, MN: Heinemann (2011).

Learn More Online

To learn more about harbor seals, visit
www.bearportpublishing.com/ADayAtTheBeach

About the Author

Ellen Lawrence lives in the United Kingdom. Her favorite books to write are those about nature and animals. In fact, the first book Ellen bought for herself when she was six years old was the story of a gorilla named Patty Cake that was born in New York's Central Park Zoo.

Answers

Page 7: Scientists use harbor seals' spotty fur patterns as a way to tell individuals apart and keep track of their behavior.

Page 22:

1. The pup is begging its mother for milk.

2. The seal is hunting for food on the seabed.

3. Seals get all the water they need from the juicy fish and other animals they eat.